Indian CUISINE

Enslow PUBLISHING

COOKING WITH CULTURE

BY JENNIFER LOMBARDO

Please visit our website, www.enslow.com. For a free color catalog of all our high-quality books, call toll free 1-800-398-2504 or fax 1-877-980-4454.

Library of Congress Cataloging-in-Publication Data
Names: Lombardo, Jennifer, author.
Title: Indian cuisine / Jennifer Lombardo.
Description: Buffalo, New York : Enslow Publishing, 2025. | Series: Cooking with culture | Includes index.
Identifiers: LCCN 2024002179 | ISBN 9781978540392 (library binding) | ISBN 9781978540385 (paperback) | ISBN 9781978540408 (ebook)
Subjects: LCSH: Cooking, Indic–Juvenile literature. | Food–India–Juvenile literature. | LCGFT: Cookbooks.
Classification: LCC TX724.5.I4 L66 2025 | DDC 641.5954–dc23/eng/20240212
LC record available at https://lccn.loc.gov/2024002179

Published in 2025 by
Enslow Publishing
2544 Clinton Street
Buffalo, NY 14224

Portions of this work were originally authored by Mary Molly Shea and published as *Foods of India*. All new material in this edition authored by Jennifer Lombardo.

Designer: Leslie Taylor
Editor: Caitie McAneney

Photo credits: Cover (photo) norikko/Shutterstock.com; Series Art (background icon pattern) porcelaniq/Shutterstock.com; Series Art (series logo) lukeruk/Shutterstock.com; p. 5 Indian Food Images/Shutterstock.com; p. 7 Mazur Travel/Shutterstock.com; p. 9 Timolina/Shutterstock.com; p. 11 Bartosz Luczak/Shutterstock.com; p. 13 ab1358/Shutterstock.com; p. 15 StockImageFactory.com/Shutterstock.com; p. 17 sunil ck/Shutterstock.com; p. 19 CR3 PHOTO/Shutterstock.com; p. 21 (chai) sdx15/Shutterstock.com, (lassi) Alphonsine Sabine/Shutterstock.com, (tea) Natalia Lisovskaya/Shutterstock.com.

Printed in the United States of America

CPSIA compliance information: Batch #CSENS25: For further information contact Enslow Publishing at 1-800-398-2504.

Contents

Words in the glossary appear in **bold** type the first time they are used in the text.

Into India

India is one of the most **diverse** countries on Earth! It has the second-largest population of any country and is home to many languages, **religions**, and ways of life. The cuisine found in India is just as diverse as its people! A place's cuisine includes both the ways foods are cooked and the dishes that are prepared.

FOOD FOR THOUGHT

INDIA HAS MANY DIFFERENT REGIONS, OR AREAS, INCLUDING MOUNTAINS, DESERTS, AND RIVERS. REGIONS HAVE THEIR OWN CUISINE BASED ON WHAT FOODS WERE AVAILABLE TO THE PEOPLE LIVING THERE.

Indian food has a long history, with the beginnings of some dishes dating back to ancient times.

From spicy to mild and **savory** to sweet, Indian cuisine has lots of **flavor**, no matter what kind you try.

The Makeup of a Meal

Indian meals have several parts. Grains are a big part of any meal in India, but the grains used are different from place to place.

In eastern and southern India, people eat rice. In other regions of India, people eat bread. In the north and northwest, wheat is harvested, ground, and made into a flatbread called chapati. A grain called pearl millet, or bajra, is a main crop in western India. It, too, can be made into bread.

In India, a clay oven is called a tandoor. Bread (and other food) baked in a tandoor is called tandoori.

FOOD FOR THOUGHT

MOST INDIANS EAT TWO OR THREE MEALS A DAY.

Keep It Meatless

Bread and rice are often eaten with beans, peas, or lentils. These are cooked into dishes called dals. For those who can afford it, yogurt may be eaten as well. If available, vegetables, fruits, and milk are added to the meal.

FOOD FOR THOUGHT

THE WORD DAL MEANS LENTILS, BEANS, OR PEAS. IT ALSO MEANS THE DISH MADE WITH THESE **INGREDIENTS**. DALS ARE MADE DIFFERENTLY FROM ONE REGION OF INDIA TO ANOTHER.

dal with lentils

Most Indians don't eat meat often. Meat dishes are saved for special **celebrations**. Indians who are **Hindu** never eat beef. **Muslim** Indians don't eat pork. Fish, however, is commonly eaten in places near the coast.

A Mix of Spices

The many spices used in Indian food make it flavorful and delicious! However, spices aren't added only for flavor. Many are also thought to make people healthier. In India, pepper is believed to aid stomach illnesses. A spice called cardamom is said to help fever and headaches.

butter chicken curry

A basic curry or masala mix includes turmeric. This makes it look yellow. Cumin, coriander, and red pepper are also commonly part of a **traditional** masala.

In India, a mix of spices is called a masala. The mix is added to liquids such as water, cream, or vinegar and blended into a sauce.

FOOD FOR THOUGHT

THE INGREDIENTS IN A MASALA DIFFER FROM REGION TO REGION. IN OTHER COUNTRIES, BOTH THE SPICE MIX AND THE SPICY DISH ITSELF MAY BE CALLED CURRY.

From the North

The state of Punjab is in northern India. Most Indian restaurants in western countries such as the United States serve Punjabi dishes.

Northern India has hot summers and cold winters. Fruits and vegetables grow well in many areas. People in this region eat chapati as their main food. Bread called naan is also served.

FOOD FOR THOUGHT

DRIED FRUITS, NUTS, AND DAIRY PRODUCTS ARE ALSO ADDED TO NORTHERN INDIAN DISHES.

The northern Indian dish shown here is called *saag*. It's made with leafy green vegetables. This picture is saag paneer. Paneer is a mild Indian cheese.

Some Indian breads are flat, like chapati, while others use yeast to rise, like naan. Samosas are bread "pockets" with meat or vegetables inside.

Pickle It!

The parts of India that are covered by desert don't often have fresh fruits and vegetables. So, people in western India **pickle** the fruits and vegetables on hand to make them last longer. These pickled foods are called achar.

To the south of the desert is the big city of Mumbai. It's on the west coast of India. There, fishers bring in many kinds of seafood. Head further south, and you'll find a spicy dish called vindaloo!

FOOD FOR THOUGHT

VINDALOO CONSISTS OF MEAT, VINEGAR, AND CHILI PEPPERS. ITS RED COLOR HINTS AT THE DISH'S VERY SPICY FLAVOR.

Pickled Mango

Ingredients

five to seven green mangoes,
  hard and not yet ripe
1/2 tablespoon fenugreek seeds
1/3 cup mustard seeds
1/3 cup red chili powder
2 1/2 tablespoons turmeric powder
1/2 cup sea salt
at least 3 cups mustard oil

Equipment

a clean, dry jar
knife
spoon
bowl
some way to **grind** your spices,
  such as a spice grinder
measuring cups and spoons

Be sure to have an adult help you cut up the mango, grind the spices, and follow the steps.

Steps

1. Allow the fenugreek and mustard seeds to dry by sitting in the sun for a couple hours or **dry roasting**. Grind together.
2. Mix these and the other spices in a big bowl.
3. Chop the green mango into bite-sized chunks.
4. Mix the mango into the spices. Coat them completely.
5. Put the spices and mango into the jar. Pour 1 cup of mustard oil over the mixture. Close the lid.
6. Store in a sunny spot for a few days, stirring every day. (Bring to a cool place at night.) Or, if it's not sunny, put it in a cool, dry place and let sit for a few extra days, again stirring every day.
7. Pour in the rest of the mustard oil. Keep the jar in a cool, dry place for about a week. Then, taste it!

Southern States

Southern India is bordered by water, with the Bay of Bengal to the east and the Arabian Sea to the west. In this region, cooks use fish and coconut in their dishes. In the center of the southern region, a spice called tamarind creates an almost sour taste in dishes.

To the west, people eat lamb stew and steamed rice-and-lentil cakes called *idli*. Also common are *dosas*, which are pancakes made of rice and lentils that are stuffed with vegetables.

Dosas have been served in South Asia for a thousand years at least! They were made thicker in the past, though.

FOOD FOR THOUGHT

CHUTNEY MAY BE SERVED WITH DOSAS. CHUTNEY IS A SWEET AND SPICY MIX OF FRUITS.

India's East

Huge crops of rice, vegetables, and fruit grow in eastern India. Near the Bay of Bengal, it's common to mix rice and fish. The hilsa fish is sometimes wrapped in pumpkin leaves before it's cooked. Further from the coast, pork is a popular meat. Bamboo shoots are sometimes used in preparing food as well.

FOOD FOR THOUGHT

DESSERTS SUCH AS *SANDESH* ARE AN IMPORTANT PART OF BENGALI CELEBRATIONS.

There are different words for rice in the more than 20 official languages of India.

Eastern India is well known for its sweets too. *Rosogollas* are treats made of milk, flour, sugar, and rose water. Sandesh is made from sugar, pistachio nuts, and paneer.

Drink Up

No meal is complete without a drink! In northern and eastern India, tea is common. Coffee is more common in southern India.

An Indian drink called chai mixes black tea, cream, and the spices of cinnamon, cardamom, clove, and ginger. Together, these make a creamy, sweet drink that has become popular worldwide. Lassi is a sugary yogurt drink, and Indian soda mixes a fizzy drink with lime and salt.

chai

Are you ready to try the diverse cuisine of India?

lassi

tea

FOOD FOR THOUGHT

FRUIT JUICES (MANGO, GUAVA, AND OTHER FRUITS) AND COCONUT MILK ARE ALSO POPULAR DRINKS IN INDIA.

Glossary

celebration: An event held in honor of an occasion.

diverse: Differing from each other.

dry roast: To cook over a hot fire without a fat like oil.

flavor: A feature of a food or drink that gives it a special taste.

grind: To make into tiny pieces or powder.

Hindu: A follower of Hinduism, a major religion of south Asia.

ingredient: A part of a mixture.

Muslim: A follower of the religion of Islam.

pickle: To add a mixture of vinegar or salt to a food to make it last longer.

religion: Belief in and way of honoring a god or gods.

savory: A taste that is spicy or salty, but not sweet.

traditional: Having to do with long-practiced customs.

For More Information

Books

Lowe, Lindsay. *Indian Culture and Cooking*. London, UK: Brown Bear Books, 2024.

Tracy, Kathleen. *Indian*. Hollywood, FL: Mason Crest Publishers, 2023.

Websites

India Country Profile
kids.nationalgeographic.com/geography/countries/article/india
Learn more about the country of India with National Geographic for Kids.

India: Rice
asiasociety.org/korea/rice-india
Find out more about rice in India and in other Asian cultures here.

Publisher's note to educators and parents: Our editors have carefully reviewed these websites to ensure that they are suitable for students. Many websites change frequently, however, and we cannot guarantee that a site's future contents will continue to meet our high standards of quality and educational value. Be advised that students should be closely supervised whenever they access the internet.

Index